When I Am Weak, Then I Am Strong

Linnea Quyen

BookLeaf Publishing

India | USA | UK

Presentation by *BookLeaf Publishing*

Web: www.bookleafpub.com

E-mail: info@bookleafpub.com

ISBN: 9789360941413

First edition 2024

I want to dedicate this book to my husband, Stephen, first and foremost, who loved me before I truly knew how to love all of myself. To my brother and sister who have always had my back and been the strongest support system a person could have. To my daughter, Mayli, who blesses me each day, showing me the beauty and joy in living fully authentic, moment to moment. To my parents for their sacrifices, continued support and loving care that I could be where I am today. To my mother-in-law who loves me as her own and has one of the biggest, most giving and caring hearts I know. To the individuals who have befriended Stephen and I along the way and taken us in like family. To our church families who continue to strengthen and uplift me in my walk with God, showing me I never have to go it alone. To each person who has believed in me, whether as an individual, a daughter of God and/or in my ability to do something with the words that come to me late at night. Thank you

And lastly, but most importantly, to God. For this life. For lovingly guiding and transforming it into something only You could make. Thank You

I love each and every one of you.

The Greatest Communion Lies in the Sharing of Our Broken

I need to let go of trying to oust what makes me feel uncomfortable. For that is my broken... the places that make me feel uncomfortable.

Being called a whore and a slut in high school hurt deeply. It messed up my thinking, way of processing. Made me overly anxious and overthink everything. I was so afraid of becoming those labels that every action I took, every word I spoke, every gesture I made, I did very cautiously and consciously. I was even afraid to walk with my back straight to keep my bottom from moving in any way as I had been called a "butt whore" when I walked normally. Even though I hadn't actually done anything wrong, I was afraid to be myself. My voice and sense of self got lost. On top of that, the individuals who I thought were my friends labeled me those as well and left me. I was alone in my heartache. That it has continued to pop up in other experiences and ways in my life since then has been discouraging at times.

But it is a part of me. There is no need to try to oust it. What if this broken wasn't meant to be overcome per se, but *used?* Given. To give a voice to this kind of lost, this kind of broken.

To say, "Yes, I've been here and you're not alone. I'm with you. It hurts, this suffering. This pain, numbness, block. But I want you to feel into it. It wasn't meant to be blocked, tucked away, 'patched up' and hung in the depths of the mind out of fear, where your hope is that no one can find it and you're never likely to think about it.

The greatest communion lies in the sharing of the brokenness. The strength lies in being vulnerable, trusting others with your wounds."

Like author Ann Voskamp of "The Broken Way" says, "It's always the vulnerable heart that breaks broken hearts free." I am not a victim of what happened to me in high school. I will use my voice to break others free from their mind encapsulation.

This is what happened and this is how it shaped me. I don't need to try to oust anything. God is using what is there to continually shape me into how He sees me, shape me back into how I was

made. In Love. And that is how and who I am,
and Whose I am.

"It's Okay to Make Noise"

It wasn't until just a few years ago while I was caregiving for an older woman, that I realized I didn't need to always be so quiet to seem respectful. That wasn't an expectation. Not a realistic one anyway.

She said, "It's okay to make noise" after I was trying hard to step around items on the ground and ended up tripping over something anyway that made a big noise. But it was quite a revelation. It didn't feel like she was just talking about that moment then and there, but for all of my life.

"It's okay to make noise" also meant to me, "It's okay to be heard, be seen. It's okay to take up space. It's okay to make mistakes, too." But is making noise a mistake? Perhaps, in this case, it was. In general though, a noise, a sound is not necessarily a mistake. It can be an intention. For a need, a want, a desire. It's your voice, and I think I have been discovering mine more and more since then.

The Instagram account "Raising Yourself" got me reflecting about how I was raised to be "good" and how it came at the cost of self-love, embracing everything that makes me me, and letting myself be all of who I am. We are not obligated to be what our parents expect or hope for us to be. It said, "The most important thing you can be when you grow up is yourself."

Let me be clear, this doesn't mean I don't love my parents. I do, wholeheartedly. They have been doing the best they can with how they were raised, what they have been given, with the best of intentions. But as Maya Angelou says, "When you know better, do better." That is what I am seeking to do. They are, too ♡

It has been an uncovering, discovering and healing journey, even more so since having Mayli. I want to do this for her as much as for myself and liberate us from a damaging cycle. Let it be known to her that she is free and safe to embrace and be all of who she is.

Forgiven

Two things about God. He is big on answering prayer and on forgiving. When you have done everything you can about a situation and are left in a most weakened state - kneeling, crying out, pleading, desperate for an answer.. even desperate for Him - He will kneel down and meet you right where you are.

"Then you will call on me and come and pray to me, and I will listen to you. You will seek me and find me when you seek me with all your heart. 'I will be found by you,' declares the Lord, 'and will bring you back from captivity.'" (Jeremiah 29: 12-14)

He will release us from our own imprisonment, in whatever form it is present in.

(Isaiah 43:25) I, I am He who blots out your transgressions for my own sake, and I will not remember your sins.

From refraining to carry another's transgressions
in mind, one is not risking the tainting of the
mind and heart, keeping them innocent and pure.
This also prevents judgment and condemnation
from taking place. It provides space needed for
curiosity, contemplation, grace and compassion
to seep in in order for understanding, repentance,
healing and mending to take place.

God does this for us.

We are called to live this way for one another -
blotting out any and all transgressions, inequities
and impurities, and forgiving them; choosing to
recognize ourselves and one another only as a
reflection of God: holy, innocent, and pure; and
having our hearts open to be upholding, bearing
in and enduring each other's suffering, pain and
burdens (Galatians 6:2) that they would be seen
through to the other side - in that the love of God
would be witnessed and fulfilled for His glory.

...

You and I don't have to keep ourselves prisoner -
with shame, fear, doubt or anything else - of
things of the past that continue to show up in the
present. God wants to free us. He *has* already

freed us, in overcoming the world (John 16: 33). Hallelujah! We are victorious (Romans 8: 37).

...

Thank You for Your forgiveness, God. That we can break free the chains of anything and everything.

Rediscovering My Innocence and Joy

I remember always looking back at a photo of myself on my sixth birthday as I got older, wondering if I would ever feel that way again. In the picture, I am with my older sister and have my hair in a bob. But it is something about the innocence and pure joy in my face as I'm standing there, beaming into the camera, that captures me.

I never thought I would find that innocence again, especially after the degradative labeling in high school. Innocence and joy felt like things that were going to be memories from then on.

But today - Joy. Experiencing joy.. that was what I felt led to. "Grace" and "Compassion" were words that popped into mind. I was ready to think "Love" next when "Joy" came in instead.

I was surprised but realized it was true. I take the time to be very intentional about giving grace/being gracious, being compassionate, being and giving love. But I don't usually stop to think about or feel joy. Not intentionally

anyway. So I thought, "Why not?" I remembered
author Alex Elle of "How We Heal," saying part
of healing is feeling joy as well. Not just trying
to re/navigate and recover from the past/trauma.

God has been a significant part of my healing.
Without Him, I don't think I would be able to
rediscover innocence or pure joy within myself.

I felt and experienced them today, was made
more aware of opportunities for them through
Mayli. Like cape-flying with her blanket while
singing, flopping backwards onto a bouncy
mattress (try it. It's fun :), or spinning and
running fast in circles as ways of dancing. Her
laugh, that secretive side grin, the way she runs
to me, runs up to me to be picked up, the way
she pulls me in and wraps her arms tightly
around me that makes me feel so deeply bonded
to her, the way she carefully positions herself to
sit snuggled right up against me when I'm
already sitting down... That girl brings me all
kinds of joy. Her innocence brings out mine.

I thank God every day for the blessing that she
is. The blessing He gifted me with.

Thank you for helping me find and reconnect
with more of myself, Baby Girl. The part that

wants to be goofy, fun-loving and carefree. The
part that wants to know she will be loved no
matter what might go awry. The Inner Child me.
I love you, forever and always. ♡

Connective Love

Love. Felt so much Love, God, connection this morning as I was prayerfully meditating and by myself in the darkness in the kitchen that, at one point, I just put my arms out to receive it all and felt God's presence glowing directly at me. Like I could almost see His face.

By "connection," I mean feeling a sort of deep, emotional bonding with others I haven't felt in a very, very long time.

It started when I learned the dad of one of my cousin's childhood friends (who became family) passed, and I chose to reach out to his daughter. Our conversation back and forth was meaningful. What her and her family went through made me want to show that they are being thought of, share warmth and love, and give to those who need it most. The flower arrangement I chose, I felt her dad's presence in.

The incident also made me feel this sense of urgency to connect with my parents more. That has turned out well, too. Somehow getting an unexpected, heartfelt apology from my mom for childhood disciplining through spanking. My parents connecting more with family members and friends they would not have thought to or felt a need to till a later time.

In our small Bible study group, I finally, somehow, found my voice and was able to share my thoughts without too much doubt at all. It felt like it was coming from the heart space. And other people could relate to it, surprisingly...

I feel more connected to God, to how to love others and be with them in a way that makes them feel loved.

Also, with our pets. Our cat, Bebe, dealt with so much in the past two plus months. I feel like the neglect I was giving her was also a reflection of my own self-care. I wasn't choosing her until it was getting late when the maggots appeared from botfly larvae unbeknownst to us, and I didn't have a choice but to. Then her pee kept being red, bloody. It was the stones.

That is when it really hit me. I needed to choose her. Otherwise, she would keep fading. And I was ready to choose her. I told her I love her and for the first time, in a long while, really meant it. I petted her softly and spent time with her. I

wanted to be with her. She is one of the sweetest
beings I have had the fortune of having in my
life and befriending. Our dog, Benji, too.

Do I Love Myself

Do I love myself?

Very rarely do I ask this or feel a need to inquire.
I am not sure why. It is actually a pertinent
question. My level of mental health/stability
could be gauged by this.

But tonight was different. After I had finished
brushing my teeth in the restroom, I felt a pull to
look at my reflection in the mirror straight in the
eyes (which also happens seldom). What I saw
and felt were different. There was a certainty, a
knowingness about myself, and a light in my
eyes that hadn't been there before.

Something in my head decided to ask then and
there, "Do I love myself?" Without skipping a
beat, my inner voice answered, "I do. A lot!" I
felt such a surge of joy inside. It made me beam
into the mirror. Had I finally reconnected with
my six-year-old self?

This is a rare moment for me. One to take note
of. I cannot say experiencing joy and having

love for myself have come easy. It's been a long,
sought-out but ever so worth it of a journey.

A Mind Conglomerate to Love

I started my personal blog in 2019, when my mental health took its deepest plunge as of yet (refer to "On 'Retard' and Intrusive Thoughts"), with the intention of discovering what Agape Love is, what that meant for and in my life, and how it would impact/affect my life mentally, emotionally, physically, socially and spiritually. This was with the hope that such love would gradually lead me to become a fully healed, self-aware and more loving and compassionate Being.

The title of the blog, "A Mind Conglomerate to Love," encompasses all the mind thoughts, little tidbits, I have had throughout my journey with God. Reading them, they might seem jumbled, incomplete, uncertain, and/or have progress one moment then go backwards another, hence the "conglomerate." However, together, they are meant to convey the progression of my thoughts, feelings and experience as I have, hopefully and only by the Holy Spirit, been led closer to what this Love truly is.

I hadn't felt like I had reached this in full or at least had a deep, significant, defining moment, until I finally could declare, without any doubt, that I do love myself. It feels like it has finally come full circle. But I know God isn't done just yet. (Continue to use me as a vessel, Lord. 🙏)

"You are a Light unto my feet. You make my paths straight. Though I may stumble, I will not fall, for You are with me." (Psalm 119: 105, Psalm 37: 23-24)

No More Compartmentalizing My Faith

At the women's retreat "Never the Same." I slept on the couch in the breakroom of the Brundage cottage (which is where I'm writing from currently) because the snoring in the room was too much for me to fall asleep to, even with my rain white noise on. But then someone in the upstairs room went to the restroom and flushed, and it woke me up. But that's okay. Time for reflection :)

Yesterday's evening session on getting out of comfortableness, taking risks when Jesus calls us to, and therefore, rocking the boat, led me to the realization that I cannot continue to and do not need to be compartmentalizing who I share my faith with.

On Facebook, I openly share as there are Stephen's family who believe in God and a good amount of Jesus-following people I am friends with on there. But on Instagram, I have been editing or leaving out the more God/faith parts or just leaving out God's and Jesus' names on what I share publicly to make it more mainstream, less uncomfortable for whoever sees it because I know there are very few Jesus-followers who I am friends with on there.

But at the expense of sharing Jesus for fear of rocking the boat. For fear of losing friends who I dearly care for but know they don't have belief or much care in Jesus and God alike. So I guess I have been trying to spare their feelings.

But that is not what Jesus wants from me. He wants *All* of me. He doesn't want me to be afraid of sharing Him. He doesn't want me to be afraid of rejection from man. After all, He is the one who openly accepted me and took me in. Who immediately reached out, chose me, saved me, called me His. He is the one who will *never* reject me, who has never rejected me. Why should it matter how man perceives me for following Jesus, who loves me so deeply and without conditions? It ought not to.

That is what Jesus placed on my heart and soul last night.

Sing Like Never Before

 "Bless the Lord, oh my soul. Oh-oh-oh my soul. Worship His holy name. *Sing like never before,* oh my soul. I'll worship Your holy name." (10, 000 Reasons)

These song lyrics just came into my head out of nowhere and I started singing them. I never thought much about the phrase "sing like never before" or felt a feeling to think on it until just now.

Singing like never before perhaps means feeling the words within your whole being like never before. Where they have such immense meaning when they didn't before. They melt your soul. You are so deeply touched and moved by them. You feel God's grace penetrating your heart. You feel His unending Love for you. It wraps its arms around you and you find yourself falling, relaxing into them. You're so moved, it brings you to tears of thankfulness. Gratitude. For everything God is and has done for you. And of joy for this healing He has brought you to and depth of Love you are coming to grasp and experience more and more of because of and through Him.

That is just what I felt as we were singing altogether last night during the women's retreat, when the worship leader stopped playing the keyboard and the whole congregation could be heard singing. It was beautiful. It was angelic. Especially as we were singing a song with the words "holy holy holy." They felt so sacred to sing. I closed my eyes and could feel it.

Benji

You've been the goodest boy. Thank you for teaching me more about kindness for others in the way that you are. I will always remember your loving squeaks at various times. The first when you saw us leaving the shelter after we'd met you and knew we wanted you but couldn't take you with us the initial day. Another time when the baby squirrels had fallen out of their home high up in a tree into our yard. We wouldn't have been able to at least try to rescue them if it hadn't been for those squeaks alerting us. Then when we first brought Mayli home ♡

You have been so so loving and so so gentle. Always curious, determined to explore everything outside. Basking in the sun as much as possible. Rolling around in the grass. Zooming in circles around the yard. Mayli loved watching that! It always made her laugh. Crossing your front legs most times when lying down. Licking the couch cover. Howling! She enjoyed that and joining in on it, too. And at the tail end, finally finding your true voice/bark. ...

I am so sorry I wanted and tried to take that
away from you, honestly thinking your barking
with the neighbor dog was a bother to our
neighbors. I will never do that again or care
what our neighbors might think. I hope you can
forgive me for that.. It was relieving to hear you
bark again and make other noises trying to
communicate with the other dogs last Tuesday.

Thank you for gracing us with your presence,
your uplifting spirit these past six or so years.
We love you so so much. You have been such a
joy. It has been an honor and blessing to have
you in our lives. ♡ May God take you into His
doggy kingdom as peacefully and lovingly as
possible. 🙏

Sense of Life Renewed

Signs of Life, even amidst death and sorrow.

We retraced Benji's and our footsteps out at Seven Mile Slough yesterday where we were less than two weeks ago after learning about his lymphoma diagnosis.

He had stood in the trench then and there had only been water running through. Most of the leaves had still been on the trees.

I stood staring into the trench yesterday and couldn't believe my eyes. It was filled with leaves upon leaves of every crimson autumn color. Every tree was barren. Every tree had dropped every one of its leaves. I looked up to the sky and breathed it in - the Richness and resounding sense of Life. Life renewed. And I knew Benji was there with us. His presence filled the air.

On "Retard" and Intrusive Thoughts

I think many, if not all of us, can agree that being misrepresented, misunderstood, and mis-seen can be a struggle to handle and is painful.

I remember the first time I experienced having a thought that was not true and having no idea where it was coming from or why it kept repeating itself. "I peed myself." I was on an airplane next to a woman older than myself. After we got off, she reunited with other people on the plane she knew, and I overheard her say she had sat next to someone who was retarded. Hmm. That was not true of me. But then what of that thought that kept repeating itself?

Little did I know that after a long tumble down a hill where I blacked out momentarily while skiing not long before this plane ride would lead to a chemical imbalance in my brain. I began hearing voices clearly outside of my head, even having conversations with them that would lead to insomnia, and thoughts like the repeating one that I came to know as intrusive thoughts. This was in 2019, the deepest plunge my mental health has taken as of yet.

Since then, I have been on medication that took away the voices and have kept the intrusive thoughts more at bay. The range of these thoughts has since expanded, including words and phrases from incidents as well as other people that became internalized. These tend to get more frequent and loud/intrusive when I am experiencing higher-than-usual levels of stress, anxiety, fear, shame, anger, agitation and/or doubt. At times, I feel like other people can hear them and believe I am truly thinking that thought. Therefore, I must be "_(insert label/phrase/belief)_," they think.

But I wanted to take a moment to raise awareness on intrusive thoughts as it is a silent internal happening a person experiences, seems weird for any person to be experiencing, and so does not get much attention in the mental health realm.

A person's intrusive thoughts do *not* define who they are in any way. I can assure you they do not actually want to be thinking the intrusive thought they have. It is not something they/I/we have control over.

All this to say, take a moment to pause and
really think about what words you are choosing
to say about any situation, person or alike before
deciding to say them. Be careful not to judge a
book by its cover or even the first few pages.
Make a conscious effort to look deeper every
moment you have.

Thank you ♡ 🙏

Also, for those experiencing intrusive thoughts,
you are not alone. I see you. I am with you. I am
one of you. They are difficult to navigate but not
impossible. You are way more than what they
say to you and/or about you. Much, much more.
I promise 🖤

To Love Fully Without Fear of the Past

Realized tonight my deepest fear. During Communion earlier in the day, what caught my throat and broke me into tears as I looked down at the piece of bread in my left hand and the small cup of red juice in my right is, *what if I am never able to let myself love fully, and thereby never experience the love God intends for us to have for one another to its deepest and fullest, because of my fear of the past repeating itself if I do?* That what happened in my past, the labels I was given for it despite being innocent, won't find and take hold of me again. That if I put my whole heart into knowing, loving and caring for people unconditionally, it won't somehow turn around and condemn and shame me. Especially from the people who I have grown fond of in church and elsewhere. That would really hurt...

I am reminded: "There is no fear in love, but Perfect Love casts out all fear." (1 John 4:18)

...

Going through something as complex as I have
been made me feel like it was too risky to bring
to God. But I knew I had to. "How do I even
begin to pray for this?" I wagered out loud.

Inner turmoil and heightened intrusive thoughts
related to the situation began taking a toll on my
mental stability. I attempted to separate my
feelings from truths in the Bible but still felt a
sense of defeat and pain inside... Though my
head knows nothing can separate me from the
love of God, my heart was still fearful I would
lose His love.

It got to the point where I was inwardly spiraling
in confusion and darkness that God led me to the
word "acceptance." That has changed
everything.

It made me relearn that I can accept and love
myself just as I am, right in this moment. What I
have been struggling with has been making it
really difficult to choose acceptance of myself.
But in accepting what I feel, that I feel the way I
feel and that that cannot be controlled no matter
how hard I try to push it away brought relief. It
also took out fear I was having over what I was
feeling.

God accepts me, accepts us just as we are, no matter what the present moment carries. You do not have to work to earn this acceptance. It just is. That's how He is.

Over the past few days, He has also assured my heart that He sees me and does understand what I am going through. That it can and will be figured out together. He will rescue me from this trouble (Psalm 34: 17-19). I don't have to live in fear of it. He is with me. Not only does He accept me, but He will continue to love me through this. ..In Perfect Love. ..which I am beginning to feel is synonymous with Unconditional Love.

I was afraid I would be brought back to past shame and labeling, but, in fact, this has released me from those altogether.

As for the intrusive thoughts, I realized I need to accept them as well, no matter how uncomfortable they may make me. Not try to keep them down and away, but acknowledge them, prayerfully breathe through them, and send love and compassion to them when they arise, resting in the assurance that they are not true of myself nor the situation. They want to be,

and need to be, released from my mind, body
and nervous system, otherwise they will remain
trapped in me in some way until another
situation brings them out again... I believe God
wants me to be fully healed from them.

...

Thank You for this Perfect Unconditional Love
that we can receive and experience from You,
God. That casts every fear away. 🙏 It is more
than enough. It is more than I deserve... and yet,
You know it is everything I need. We need. It is
our Saving Grace. ♡

It Always Comes Back to Our Innocence

It always comes back to our innocence. How innocent we feel about ourselves. How capable we are of accepting ourselves when we don't feel as innocent that leads us back to that innocence. Every time.

You take a fall you don't think you can come back from. Make a mistake your mind holds you hostage to. Have something new, worrisome, deep and/or heavy that you feel you cannot talk about. An unspoken. Something you are even afraid to bring to your closest confidant. Suddenly, the innocence you had as a child feels blotched. Again. You are left uncertain about the sense of uprightness within you. You are left raw. Exposed. - Too exposed. Darkness, shame, fear fester and eat at you from inside. You feel alone in it, in this pit, with no way out.

Please. Don't let it stop you from believing in yourself. "It's not that you've made a mistake. You're learning," a voice tells me. You are innocent. Have faith in yourself. Have patience with yourself. There is good in you.

There is Hope. You are made in the Image of
The One who created you. In Perfect Love. With
Grace and Compassion poured out onto and over
you. No matter what. Nothing can separate you
from these Truths.

God will never forsake you. He has never left
your side.

Bring It To The Light

Please don't ever feel ashamed for what happens to come up for you. God wants to hear about it so He can help you overcome it. Not that He doesn't already know about it, but to hear it directly from you means you are seeking His help. So He will answer. (Jeremiah 29: 13-14)

This hasn't always been my thought system, but as my trust in Him has grown, I know this is what He desires from us.

We don't need to feel like we have to go into hiding every time something that is new to us and makes us unsure and wary, and/or is potentially of sinful nature comes up. Nothing is ever too little and insignificant that He wouldn't stop to listen intently to what we have to share. Nothing is ever too much or too great for Him to handle. He equally cares for each one of us individually (1 Peter 5:7).

He is our loving Father who won't condemn us, won't forsake us. He will guide us with grace and compassion through and out to the way that

is holy, righteous and good. He has every time
for me.

"Do not fear, for I have redeemed you; I have
called you by name, you are mine. When you
pass through the waters, I will be with you; and
through the rivers, they will not overwhelm you;
when you walk through fire you will not be
burned, and the flame shall not consume you.
For I am the Lord, your God, the Holy One of
Israel, your Savior." (Isaiah 43: 1-3)

Light Amidst the Fog

My walk in the fog this morning reminded me of growing up in Washington State. Some nostalgia. Deeply in tune with nature.

I started to walk in the direction my heart felt led - towards the one hill in the park with about seven barren trees almost perfectly spaced apart from each other - as I was immersed in thought and prayer for a resolution about a new challenge with Mayli. I had reached out to a therapist friend who has a toddler right about Mayli's age about the situation, and was texting back and forth with her as I walked. It was just as I approached the base of the hill that it was resolved. Her advice calmed my heart immediately upon reading it. (Thank You for friends who are also therapists and for answering my prayer.)

One of the trees on top of the hill felt like The Tree of Life to me. I was so taken in, as if I was closer to meeting God. I stepped nearer and walked around it, trying to capture its essence from every angle.

Just then, the sun started to peek out through the
fog. It felt like God's presence, His Light,
breaking through. Something told me to stay and
watch. The sun crept behind a wisp of cloud for
a few moments before reappearing higher,
brighter, more full and vibrant.

It made me think, "That is kind of like ourselves,
isn't it?" We think maybe we have discovered
who we are. Moments of doubt, of darkness or
failure come up though, and we feel like we
have lost the intensity and integrity of who we
are. But that's where God comes in and can
redeem, restore and heal us into something we
never thought we could be. Something only He
could make. Full of light and wonder. ☀ ❄ 🔥

Embrace All You Are

Every crack.
Every fracture.
Every tear.
So more light can seep in.
So more grace, self-acceptance and Love can
pour through.

I see it in your face. Your eyes. Worn. Searching
for something.. more... Something worth holding
onto...

You are a magnificent, wondrous creation, still
in progress. With a beautiful heart, a beautiful
soul, and a beautiful mind - no matter how
messy, chaotic, confusing, lost or turbulent it
might get.

Thank You for being who You are. ♡

You are brave. It takes courage to show up every
day, every moment just as you are. Yet, you are
doing it. You can be proud of how far you have
come, where you are now, and who you have
become through it.

Embrace all you are.

The world needs you - All of you. All that you have to offer. All that you have to give - more than anything else right now.

I Will Live in Faith, not fear

"I will live in Faith, not fear," the thought from Above came through my head as I was brushing my teeth tonight.

For the longest time, I have believed Love would be the answer to the healing in ourselves and in the world. "Only Love" was my mantra. Don't get me wrong. It certainly can and does do tremendous amounts of healing. But the understanding of, and therefore, the capacity to love without God is conditionally based. At least that's how it has been for me.

To walk with, not just a seed of Faith, but a definite certainty of It that can be felt deep into the bones is electrifying. Enigmatic. It changes you from within. It empowers you.

Knowing just how loved you are by Him, no matter what darkness you endure. No matter what mistakes, accidents or unspeakables you make or have and want to hide from, want to make disappear. He will hold you up, no matter those times. He will be with you, no matter

what. You will not have to face them alone.
Ever.

"In all these things we are more than conquerors
through him who loved us. For I am convinced
that neither death, nor life, nor angels, nor rulers,
nor things present, nor things to come, nor
powers, nor height, nor depth, nor anything else
in all creation, will be able to separate us from
the love of God in Christ Jesus our Lord."
(Romans 8: 37-39)

This is a Love you can trust and hold onto, for
all your days.

Because of this Love, we are able to have the
capacity to love like Him unto ourselves and our
neighbors, and, in turn, for Him.
Unconditionally. Fully embracing. Without fear.
Without any hindrances, hesitations or doubts.

With Faith, the Love we have is powerful.
Transcendental. Even transformational.

So yes, I will live in Faith. It leads me to the
Cross. It leads me to Jesus. It leads me to the

Unfailing Love and Power over darkness and
death that are Jesus.

...

Received this Bible verse tonight:

"He who believes in me, as the Scripture has
said, from within him will flow rivers of Living
Water." (John 7:38)

There is much my mind is receiving tonight and
has been receiving. I feel like I can't stop
writing, even if it is late at night and the past
nights held little sleep.

God Must Be Known.

So I Could Stand and Sing

During worship yesterday, while singing "No Longer Slaves," I felt weight lifted off my lower back at one point and then as though I could hold, not just my back, but my whole self, straighter. Taller. Able to receive more of what God has and wants for and from me.

Our lower back region retains the fear we keep to ourselves and try to bury within. I believe what mine has been hanging onto got released.

I found myself raising my arm up while singing and fully believing, "You split the sea so I could walk right through it. My fears were drowned in Perfect Love. You rescued me so I could stand and sing, I am a Child of God."

...

In fifth grade, I remember being in the car with my sister in the passenger seat, my mom driving, and my brother and I sitting in the backseat when I said I wanted to be a singer when I grew up. Immediately, my mom shut it down, saying it wasn't realistic. I believed her.

I kept singing though because it was something where I could feel and express emotions deeply. It brought, and continues to bring, me much joy and connection with other people. But I never thought about going after that dream, that desire after she said that.

Even when a scout gave me his number and told me to call him one time when I performed at an open mic event post-college, I didn't believe it and never called. I still wonder about it sometimes...

Then Stephen and I met and a few years later moved to New Meadows, ID where we attended Church of the Nazarene in Council. The worship leader and her husband basically took us in as their own. The whole church did, but this couple especially.

She told me the story of how music had been in her life and how God used that to bring her into the worship leading role she is in now. I was so drawn in.

She was the one who saw potential in me first. We practiced songs together. I was still too anxious and frightened to sing in front of people.

One of the only solos I sang there was "You Say" by Lauren Daigle. I had to have my back turned to the congregation so I wouldn't get a panic attack. But I continued singing up there with her and the rest of the worship group on Sundays, never fully shaking off the anxiety and fear.

Stephen got a permanent job in Boise four years later where we moved into an apartment, eventually having our daughter there. We didn't attend church in person but watched the online service from Council.

A year and a half in, rent began skyrocketing outside of our budget. We decided it was time to search for a house we could afford in a town we liked. That happened to be in Emmett.

What got me back into singing was when there was a multi-church Christmas choir performance this past holiday season in town. I joined. Not only did I rediscover a passion to sing, but my heart also found a new desire to do so fully for God. To praise Him. To share the goodness He is and the hope, strength, healing and redemption we have in Him.

Whether worshipping onstage or in the pews on Sundays, or wherever and whenever I feel the desire and/or urge to, God speaks to me more and more through the words in the songs, raising my belief and trust in Him. The fear and anxieties I had before have been dissipating, losing their grip on me. The times when I am onstage, I can hold my head up and look forward at the congregation now. Thank You, God, for building my strength and belief in myself, and for turning my heart's desire of singing into an offering that can bring others closer to You.

Thank You for Everything You Are

For some reason, I felt led to read the very first post on my personal blog tonight. And I am in awe... how far God has led me. Brought life back to me and in me. I can't thank You enough. 🎶 "You're more than enough for me. Jesus, You're all I need." (Healer)

My first blog post from September 18, 2019 reads:

...I love to sing but feel I don't get chances to enough. I feel sad inside sometimes. It may or may not have to do with GAD and/or bipolar disorder. My inner soul wants to be joyous, playful and giggly. Loving, more out there, vulnerable, giving, but there's something inside that makes me refrain. ..Fear? Of rejection? Fear of something... Whatever it is, it makes it painful inside. I often feel like I have so much more to give than I really show or do. Why I hold back.. is it because it won't be good enough? I'll fail? I don't know. There's so much doubt and anxiety.

All I know is that I am to trust God. He makes me enough because He is more than enough. He calls me Beloved. This unconditional love. He gives me strength and courage. I can rest in Him. For Jesus has already saved me. He has already gone through it all and redeemed it all, that I could be redeemed. This is the way. And I do trust. I am more than this doubt, anxiety and fear. They are not who I am. God says I am His. I am made in His image of goodness, purity, holiness, love, and light. As well as held in them. This never changes. Only my feelings do, and they are impermanent. Only what remains unchanged is truth. -- God is Love. And He loves me. Nothing else needs to matter.

...

Thank You, God, for releasing all the shame, doubt, and fear and continuing to work on the anxiety in my body and mind. Thank You for giving me back Life, breathing It into me and pouring out Your Living Water into my whole being. Finding joy again when I didn't think I would. Finding grace. Finding holy, Perfect Love, connection and compassion through the knowing, feeling, seeing and sharing of brokenness. That is everything You have been and are to me. That is everything You are.

I love You. Thank You for never giving up on
me nor forsaking me. Thank You for choosing
me. Thank You for adopting me. Thank You,
that I can call myself a Child of God.

I am not worthy, yet You still want me. You fight
for me.

You. Love. Me. - Always.

That is something unfathomable. But I know
deep within my heart and whole being it is true.
So I will cling to it. Forever ♡

Thank You for saving me.

Thank You for Everything You Are 🙏

Worth Everything To Find

God is waiting for you, with arms wide open.

Cast all your burdens - fears, doubts, anxieties; everything - onto Him. All the heavy weight you were never meant to hang onto and carry alone.

"For when I am weak, then I am strong."
(2 Corinthians 12:10)

In Him.

...

Take My hand. Let Me lead you back into The Light.

Where innocence is restored.

Where joy is reclaimed.

Where the body is healed.

Where the heart and mind are renewed, at peace
and can rest easy.

Where Grace saves.

.

.

Will you join Me?

...

"...Does He think any less of me.. for it?" I
choked out. I was afraid to ask. More afraid of
what the answer would be.. But my heart needed
to know.

"No," she said. "You are loved no matter what.
This is God's Grace."

She said this with the most kind, warmhearted,
reassuring tone I had ever heard. It was reflected
in her face as well as she peered at me, gently.
The way she said it, I knew it was out of
certainty. Not just a belief but a knowing.

I about died. Though I knew these words,
hearing them this time made me immediately
bow my head, weeping in a feeling of gratitude
that was the deepest I've known.

...

Jesus is so beautifully perfect. It's kind of
breathtaking... The kindness, gentleness and love
on His face that He has for you - they are more
than you could ever fully take in... more than
you could ever imagine...

...

I love you, Jesus. I love you, God. Thank You
for the Redemptive Grace, Light and Perfect
Love we are able to receive from You, because
of You, and in You. That changes us, transforms
us, heals us from the inside out. You are
beautiful, wonderful Majesty. Worth everything
to find. ❤ 🙏 ❤